ICONS

GREECE STYLE

GREECE

Exteriors   Interiors

STYLE
Details

PHOTOS **Barbara and René Stoeltie**
EDITOR **Angelika Taschen**

TASCHEN
KÖLN LONDON LOS ANGELES MADRID PARIS TOKYO

Front cover: Laid back: sofa in Panos Alexopoulos' house on Seriphos.
Couverture: *Pour s'adosser : sofa dans la maison de Panos Alexopoulos à Seriphos.*
Umschlagvorderseite: Zum Zurücklehnen: Sofa im Haus von Panos Alexopoulos auf Seriphos.

Back cover: A glass cross: in Vassily Tseghis' house on Seriphos.
Dos de couverture: *Croix en verre : dans la maison de Vassily Tseghis à Seriphos.*
Umschlagrückseite: Ein Kreuz aus Glas: Im Haus von Vassily Tseghis auf Seriphos.

Also available from TASCHEN:

Living in Greece
200 pages
3-8228-5869-2
3-8228-5735-1 (edition with French cover)

To stay informed about upcoming TASCHEN titles, please request our magazine at www.taschen.com or write to TASCHEN, Hohenzollernring 53, D-50672 Cologne, Germany, Fax: +49-221-254919. We will be happy to send you a free copy of our magazine which is filled with information about all of our books.

Edited by Angelika Taschen, Berlin
Layout and general project management by Stephanie Bischoff, Cologne
Texts by Christiane Reiter, Berlin
Lithography by Horst Neuzner, Cologne
English translation by Pauline Cumbers, Frankfurt am Main
French translation by Anne Charrière, Croissy/Seine

Printed in Italy
ISBN 3-8228-4018-1

CONTENTS SOMMAIRE INHALT

Visitors to Greece don't always have it easy. First there's the trip there, on roads that seem to consist more of potholes than of asphalt, on board a tiny ferry lurching over and back between two islands in the Aegean, or on a propeller plane the sound of which does not really inspire confidence. And then there's the heat, the smog over Athens and the bare landscape – yet Greece is still a dream destination, a longing that never really lets you go. It is the realm of saga, myth and legend. Almost every stone exudes history and speaks of gods, warriors or philosophers. Greece is a stronghold of art and architecture, where sculptures and buildings not only keep Antiquity alive, but are ideals of beauty and harmony, now as then. It is the land of light, a light that imbues everything with that very particular splendour. "In Greece things radiate, as if their light came from within," so the sculptor Henry Moore. And Nikos Kazantzakis, world famous for his novel Zorba the Greek, said: "The light in Greece is full of spirit; such light helped man to see

THE LAND OF LIGHT
Christiane Reiter

La Grèce n'aplanit pas toujours les chemins pour ses hôtes. L'arrivée se fait par des routes plus défoncées qu'asphaltées, à bord d'un minuscule bac louvoyant entre les îles de la mer Egée, ou dans un avion à hélice dont le bruit n'inspire pas vraiment confiance. A cela peut s'ajouter la canicule, la pollution au-dessus d'Athènes et l'aridité du paysage – et pourtant ce pays reste une destination de rêve, une nostalgie lancinante qui ne nous lâche plus! Il est le royaume des légendes et des mythes, où presque chaque pierre porte la trace de l'histoire et parle des dieux, des grands guerriers, des philosophes. C'est le haut lieu de l'art et de l'architecture, où sculptures et édifices maintiennent vivant le souvenir de l'Antiquité et sont encore aujourd'hui des idéaux de beauté et d'harmonie. C'est aussi le pays de la lumière qui confère à tout et à tous cet éclat très particulier. «En Grèce, les choses rayonnent comme si leur lumière venait de l'intérieur» disait le sculpteur Henry Moore. Et de Nikos Kazantzakis, mondialement célèbre par son roman «Alexis Zorba» nous connaissons cette phrase: «La lumière en Grèce

Griechenland macht es seinen Gästen oft nicht leicht. Da ist die Anreise über Straßen, die aus mehr Schlaglöchern denn Asphalt zu bestehen scheinen, an Bord einer winzigen Fähre, die zwischen zwei Inseln der Ägäis hin- und herschlingert, oder in einer Propellermaschine, deren Geräusche kein rechtes Vertrauen erwecken. Dazu kann die Hitze kommen, der Smog über Athen oder die karge Landschaft – und dennoch ist Griechenland ein Traumziel und eine Sehnsucht, die einen nie mehr loslässt. Es ist das Reich der Sagen, Mythen und Legenden, in dem fast jeder Stein Geschichte atmet und von Göttern, Kriegsherren oder Philosophen erzählt. Es ist die Hochburg der Kunst und Architektur, in der Skulpturen und Bauten die Antike lebendig halten und damals wie heute Ideale für Schönheit und Harmonie sind. Und es ist das Land des Lichts, das allem und jedem diesen ganz besonderen Glanz verleiht. »In Griechenland strahlen die Dinge, als käme ihr Licht von innen«, sagte der Bildhauer Henry Moore einmal. Und von Nikos Kazantzakis, der mit dem Roman »Alexis Sorbas« weltberühmt wurde, stammt der Satz:

clearly." That same radiance also surrounds Greek houses. Be it the weekend refuge on Hydra, the labyrinth of small huts on Seriphos, or the idyllic farmhouse on Patmos – all these buildings are suffused with light, a sea of colours. Nowhere else can white glow as brightly and blue shine as intensely as here; complemented by shades of yellow and turquoise or pink and red nuances, reflecting the most beautiful tones of surrounding nature and at the same time providing ample scope for clear forms and basic aesthetics. The Greeks are not inclined to design that is too profuse or overloaded – instead they prefer simple arrangements of personal accessories which, like the colours, are closely bound up with the country and its people. A shell in which the sea roars, a hand-carved model of a ship, or a vase with an ancient patina: what more do you need to feel really at home?

est pleine d'esprit ; une telle lumière a aidé les gens à voir clair.»
Ce même éclat émane aussi des maisons grecques. Que ce soit
le refuge du week-end sur Hydra, le labyrinthe de petites huttes
sur Seriphos ou la maison paysanne idyllique de Patmos, toutes
ces constructions sont inondées de lumière et accueillent le jeu
des couleurs. Nulle part ailleurs le blanc peut être aussi écla-
tant, le bleu aussi intense qu'ici ; ils sont complétés par des
nuances de jaune et de turquoise ou des tons rosés à rouges,
qui reflètent les plus belles couleurs de la nature environnante et
créent en même temps un espace de formes claires à l'esthé-
tique sobre. Car les décorations chargées et débordantes sont
étrangères aux Grecs – qui préfèrent mettre en scène des
accessoires personnels en affinité, comme les couleurs, avec le
pays et ses habitants. Une conque où gronde la mer, une
maquette de bateau réalisée à la main, ou un vase patiné à
l'antique : que faut-il de plus pour vraiment se sentir chez soi ?

»Das Licht in Griechenland ist voller Geist; solches Licht half dem Menschen, klar zu sehen«. Dieser Glanz liegt auch über griechischen Häusern. Sei es das Wochenend-Refugium auf Hydra, das Labyrinth aus kleinen Hütten auf Seriphos oder das idyllische Bauernhaus auf Patmos – all diese Bauten sind licht-durchflutet und ein Spiel der Farben. Nirgendwo sonst kann Weiß so hell strahlen und Blau so intensiv leuchten wie hier; ergänzt von Gelb- und Türkisschattierungen oder Rosé- und Rottönen, die die schönsten Farben der umliegenden Natur wie-derspiegeln und zugleich Raum für klare Formen und schlichte Ästhetik lassen. Denn überquellendes und überzeichnetes Design ist den Griechen fremd – sie setzen stattdessen persön-liche Accessoires in Szene, die wie die Farben mit dem Land und seinen Menschen verbunden sind. Eine Muschel, in der das Meer rauscht, ein handgeschnitztes Schiffsmodell oder eine Vase mit antiker Patina: Was braucht man mehr, um sich wirklich zuhause zu fühlen?

"…There, at the end of the world, the earth, before it sinks into the sea, opens its arms in an embrace, forming a little harbour. On the plane between the sea and the mountains are myriad olive trees…"

Nikos Themelis, in *Anasitissi*

«…Là-bas, au bout du monde, avant de s'enfoncer dans la mer, la terre décrit un arc de ses bras, pour abriter un petit port. Dans la plaine entre mer et montagne, les oliviers sont innombrables…»

Nikos Themelis, dans *Anasitissi*

»…Dort, am Ende der Welt, macht die Erde, bevor sie ins Meer sinkt, eine Umarmung, bildet einen kleinen Hafen. In der Ebene zwischen dem Meer und den Bergen sind die Ölbäume unzählbar…«

Nikos Themelis, in *Jenseits von Epirus*

EXTERIORS

Extérieurs Aussichten

10/11 Witness to the past: The Temple of Aphaeia (c. 490 B. C.) on Aegina. *Témoin du passé : le temple d'Aphaia (vers 490 av. J.-C.) sur Egine.* Zeuge der Vergangenheit: Der Aphaia-Tempel (um 490 v. Chr.) auf Ägina.

12/13 Crystal clear: along the indented coast of Patmos. *Eau claire comme le cristal : devant la côte dentelée de Patmos.* Kristallklares Wasser: Vor der zerklüfteten Küste von Patmos.

14/15 View of the sea: a roof terrace on one of the Dodecanese islands. *Avec vue sur la mer : terrasse sur toit, dans une île du Dodécanèse.* Mit Meerblick: Eine Dachterrasse auf einer Insel der Dodekanes.

16/17 Stone decor: Jean-Claude Chalmet's cobalt blue pool on Aegina. *Ornement de pierre : donnant sur la piscine bleu cobalt de Jean-Claude Chalmet à Egine.* Steinerner Schmuck: Am kobaltblauen Pool von Jean-Claude Chalmet auf Ägina.

18/19 Fresh vitamin C: on Jean-Claude Chalmet's sunny terrace. *Vitamine C toute fraîche : sur la terrasse ensoleillée de Jean-Claude Chalmet.* Frisches Vitamin C: Auf der Sonnenterrasse von Jean-Claude Chalmet.

20/21 Favourite places: wicker chair and sofas at Jean-Claude Chalmet's house. *Places préférées : fauteuils en osier et canapés chez Jean-Claude Chalmet.* Lieblingsplätze: Korbsessel und Kanapees bei Jean-Claude Chalmet.

22/23 A view of the Peloponnese: from Audrey and Robert Browning's veranda on Hydra. *Vue jusqu'au Péloponnèse : la véranda d'Audrey et Robert Browning à Hydra.* Sicht bis zur Peloponnes: Auf der Veranda von Audrey und Robert Browning auf Hydra.

24/25 Interlocking: the house of architect Vassily Tseghis on Seriphos. *Emboîtée : la maison de l'architecte Vassily Tseghis à Seriphos.* Verschachtelt: Das Haus des Architekten Vassily Tseghis auf Seriphos.

26/27 Going up: the passage to the old "fournos"; also by Vassily Tseghis. *Marche après marche : la ruelle du vieux four, ou « ournos », également chez Vassily Tseghis.* Stufenweise: Die Gasse zum alten Ofen »fournos«; ebenfalls bei Vassily Tseghis.

28/29 Siesta in the shade: the peaceful courtyard of a house on Patmos. *Siesta à l'ombre : dans la cour d'une maison à Patmos – un calme paradisiaque.* Siesta im Schatten: Im paradiesisch ruhigen Hof eines Hauses auf Patmos.

30/31 Bathed in light: the terrace of Henri-Paul Coulon's "Pink House" on Aegina. *Plongée dans la lumière : la terrasse de la « Maison rose » d'Henri-Paul Coulon à Egine.* In Licht getaucht: Die Terrasse des »Rosa Hauses« von Henri-Paul Coulon auf Ägina.

32/33 Rocky surroundings: the cliffs of Seriphos, where Perseus beheaded Medusa. *Environnement accidenté : les rochers de Seriphos, où Persée aurait décapité Méduse.* Raue Umgebung: Die Felsen von Seriphos, wo Perseus die Medusa enthauptet haben soll.

34/35 A divine address: at the rear of the chapel on Patmos. *Adresse divine : la face arrière d'une chapelle sur Patmos.* Göttliche Adresse: Die Rückseite einer Kapelle auf Patmos.

36/37 A very personal palace: Audrey und Robert Browning's villa "Kourmada" on Hydra. *Un palais très personnel : la villa « Kourmada » d'Audrey et Robert Browning sur Hydra.* Ein ganz persönlicher Palast: Die Villa »Kourmada« von Audrey und Robert Browning auf Hydra.

38/39 Behind the mustard yellow door: Dina Nikolaou's house on Hydra. *Derrière la porte jaune moutarde : la maison de Dina Nikolaou sur Hydra.* Hinter der senfgelben Tür: Das Haus von Dina Nikolaou auf Hydra.

40/41 For friends: a cosy dining-area in front of a house on Patmos. *Pour les amis : un coin confortable devant une maison à Patmos.* Für Freunde: Eine gemütliche Essecke vor einem Haus auf Patmos.

42/43 Think pink: in front of Henri-Paul Coulon's "Pink House" on Aegina. *La vie en rose : devant la « Maison rose » Henri-Paul Coulon sur Egine.* Think Pink: Vor dem »Rosa Haus« von Henri-Paul Coulon auf Ägina.

"…A gentle bluish-green light soaked the dirty panes, seeped into the coffee house, attached itself to hands, noses and foreheads, and jumped up and down on the counter so that the bottles caught fire…"

Nikos Kazantzakis, in *Alexis Sorbas*

«…Une douce lumière bleu-vert imprégna les vitres sales, pénétra dans le café, se colla aux mains, aux nez et aux fronts, sauta sur le comptoir, et les bouteilles prirent feu…»

Nikos Kazantzakis, dans *Alexis Zorba*

»…Ein sanftes blaugrünes Licht tränkte die schmutzigen Scheiben, drang in das Kaffeehaus, hängte sich an Hände, Nasen und Stirnen und sprang auf den Schanktisch, dass die Flaschen Feuer fingen…«

Nikos Kazantzakis, in *Alexis Sorbas*

INTERIORS

Intérieurs   Einsichten

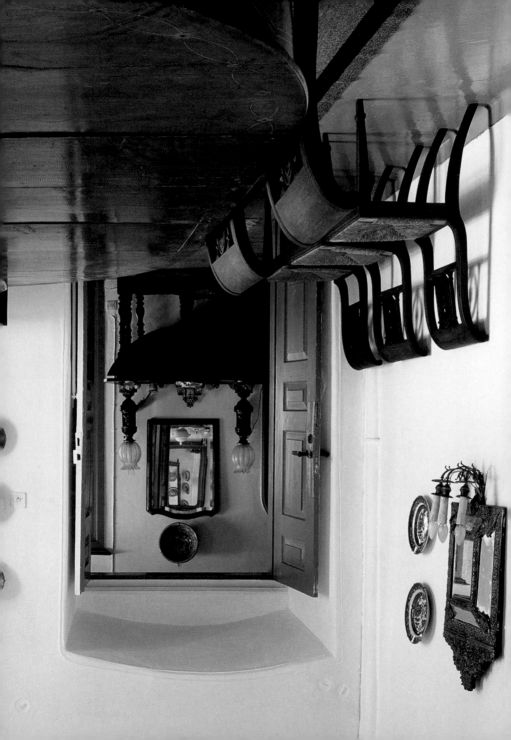

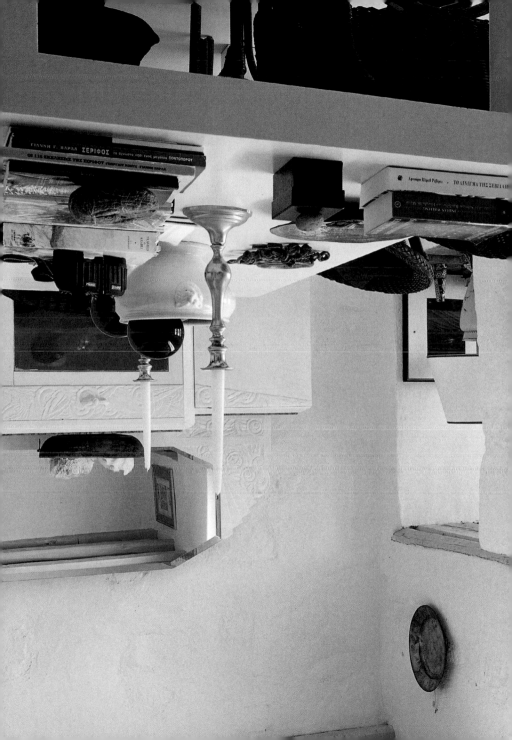

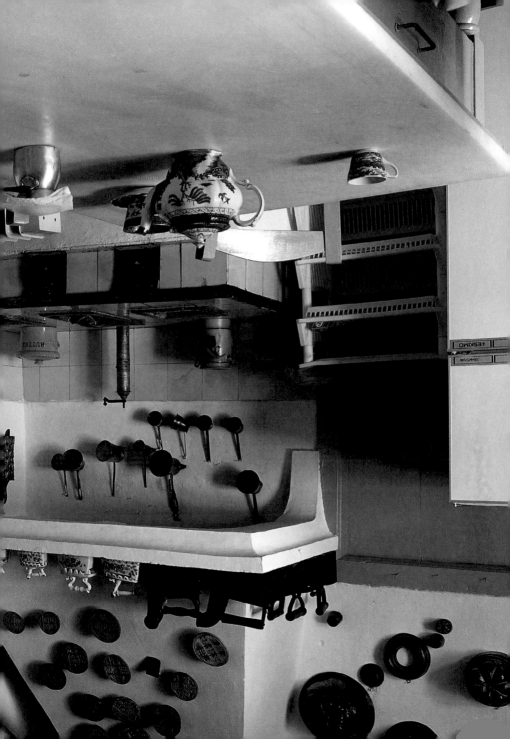

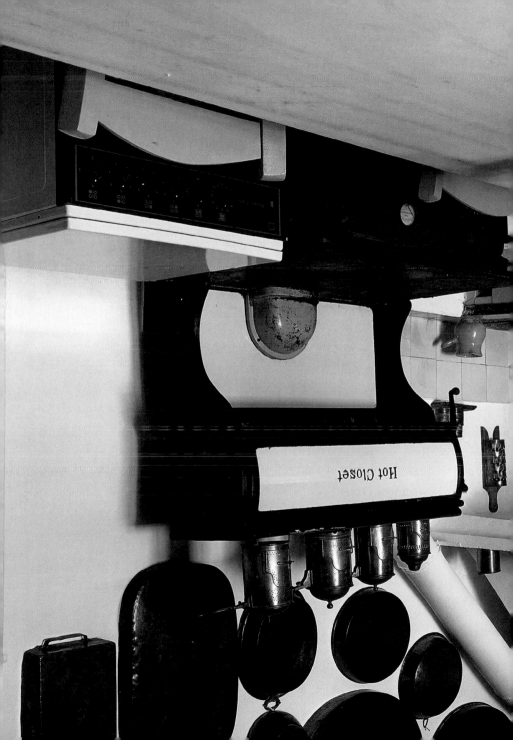

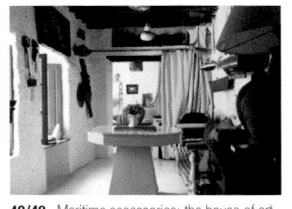

48/49 Maritime accessories: the house of art book publisher Nikos Kostopoulos. *Accessoires maritimes: dans la demeure de l'éditeur de livres d'art, Nikos Kostopoulos.* Maritime Accessoires: Im Haus des Kunstbuchverlegers Nikos Kostopoulos.

50/51 Seventh heaven: in Panos Alexopoulos' home on Seriphos. *Dormir comme au septième ciel: chez Panos Alexopoulos à Seriphos.* Schlafen wie im siebten Himmel: Bei Panos Alexopoulos auf Seriphos.

52/53 Faience table service from England: at Paouris Palace in the port of Hydra. *Service de table en faïence d'Angleterre: dans le palais Paouris, au port d'Hydra.* Fayence-Tafelservice aus England: Im Paouris-Palast am Hafen von Hydra.

54/55 High halls: in the former governor's palace on one of the Saronic islands. *Salles hautes: dans l'ancien palais du gouverneur d'une île argosaronique.* Hohe Hallen: Im ehemaligen Palast des Statthalters auf einer Argosaronischen Insel.

56/57 Orderly: the simple kitchen of a once splendid building. *Bien ordonné: la modeste cuisine de l'ancien édifice prestigieux.* Gut geordnet: In der schlichten Küche des einstigen Prachtbaus.

58/59 British style: the sitting room in "Kourmada" on Hydra. *A la manière délicate des Britanniques: le salon de la maison «Kourmada» sur Hydra.* Auf die feine englische Art: Der Salon des Hauses »Kourmada« auf Hydra.

60/61 Exhibits: a Victorian chair and valuable porcelain in "Kourmada". *Pièces d'exposition: un fauteuil victorien et de la porcelaine précieuse dans la maison «Kourmada».* Ausstellungsstücke: Ein viktorianischer Sessel und kostbares Porzellan im Haus »Kourmada«.

62/63 Turkish style: opulent sofa in Vassily Tseghis' weekend house on Hydra. *Dans le style turc: sofa généreux dans la maison de week-end de Vassily Tseghis à Hydra.* Im türkischen Stil: Üppiges Sofa im Wochenendhaus von Vassily Tseghis auf Hydra.

64/65 Shades of blue: in Vassily Tseghis' charming house on Seriphos. *Accents bleus: dans la charmante maison de Vassily Tseghis à Seriphos.* Blaue Akzente: Im charmanten Haus von Vassily Tseghis auf Seriphos.

66/67 Fireplace: the stone chimney of a house on Patmos. *Au coin du feu: la cheminée de pierre d'une maison sur Patmos.* Feuerstelle: Am steinernen Kamin eines Hauses auf Patmos.

68/69 Clear lines and geometric patterns: in Panos Alexopoulos' house on Seriphos. *Lignes claires et motifs géométriques: chez Panos Alexopoulos sur Seriphos.* Klare Linien und geometrische Muster: Bei Panos Alexopoulos auf Seriphos.

70/71 At the foot of the stairs: in Marilena Liakopoulos' marvellous house on Patmos. *Au bas de l'escalier: dans le merveilleux palais de Marilena Liakopoulos à Patmos.* Am Fuß der Treppe: Im zauberhaften Palazzo von Marilena Liakopoulos auf Patmos.

72/73 Brilliant red: window frames and coverings in Marilena Liakopoulos' sitting-room. *Rouge lumineux : cadres de fenêtres et housses dans le salon de Marilena Liakopoulos.* Leuchtendes Rot: Fensterrahmen und Bezüge im Salon von Marilena Liakopoulos.

74/75 Formal atmosphere: Dina Nikolaou's living-room on Hydra. *Ambiance formelle : le salon de Dina Nikolaou à Hydra.* Formelles Ambiente: Das Wohnzimmer von Dina Nikolaou auf Hydra.

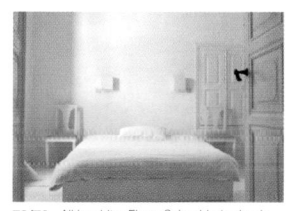

76/77 Artful kitchen: lots of space for cooking in Marilena Liakopoulos' house on Patmos. *De l'art dans la cuisine : beaucoup d'espace pour la préparation des repas chez Marilena Liakopoulos à Patmos.* Kunst in der Küche: Viel Raum zum Kochen bei Marilena Liakopoulos.

78/79 All in white: Elmar Schneider's simple bedroom on Hydra. *Tout en blanc : la modeste chambre à coucher d'Elmar Schneider à Hydra.* Ganz in Weiß: Das schlichte Schlafzimmer von Elmar Schneider auf Hydra.

80/81 On several levels: Miriam Frank's holiday home on Seriphos. *Sur plusieurs niveaux : dans la maison de vacances de Miriam Frank à Seriphos.* Auf mehreren Ebenen: Im Ferienhaus von Miriam Frank auf Seriphos.

82/83 Unusual metamorphosis on Seriphos: from an old oven to a bed. *Métamorphose inédite : ancien four à Seriphos transformé en alcôve.* Ungewöhnliche Wandlung: Aus einem alten Backofen auf Seriphos wurde ein Bett.

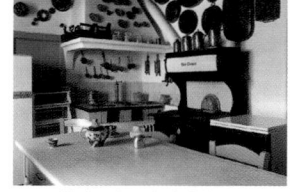

84/85 Like in a picture book: British-style kitchen at Paouris Palace on Hydra. *Comme dans un livre d'images : la cuisine aux accents britanniques du palais Paouris à Hydra.* Wie aus dem Bilderbuch: Die britisch angehauchte Küche des Paouris-Palastes auf Hydra.

86/87 Warm shades: room with a fireplace in the "Pink House" on Aegina. *Tons chauds : dans la salle de la cheminée de la « Maison rose » à Egine.* Warme Töne: Im Kaminzimmer des »Rosa Hauses« auf Ägina.

88/89 Country house flair: Maxie Leoussis' pretty kitchen on Hydra. *Air de maison de campagne : la jolie pièce-cuisine de Maxie Leoussis à Hydra.* Landhausflair: Die hübsche Wohnküche von Maxie Leoussis auf Hydra.

90/91 Art by the fireside: a wonderful spot on a cool evening. *Cheminée artistique : le plus bel endroit pour les soirées fraîches.* Kunst am Kamin: Der schönste Platz für kühle Abende.

92/93 Sunflower yellow: Vassily Tseghis' weekend house on Hydra. *Jaune tournesol : dans la maison de campagne de Vassily Tseghis à Hydra.* Sonnenblumengelb: Im Wochenendhaus von Vassily Tseghis auf Hydra.

94/95 In memory of other times: "Langada", a former farmhouse on Patmos. *Souvenir d'époques antérieures : dans l'ancienne maison paysanne « Langada » à Patmos.* Andenken an frühere Zeiten: Im ehemaligen Bauernhaus »Langada« auf Patmos.

96/97 Eastern promise: a richly ornamented living-room on one of the Dodecanese islands. *Comme au Levant : un salon richement décoré sur une île du Dodécanèse.* Wie im Morgenland: Ein reich verzierter Salon auf einer Insel der Dodekanes.

98/99 From all over the world: treasures in artist Timothy Hennessy's little house on Hydra. *Trésors du monde entier : dans le petit salon du peintre Timothy Hennessy à Hydra.* Schätze aus aller Welt: Im kleinen Salon des Malers Timothy Hennessy auf Hydra.

100/101 Hand-made: paintings and fabrics at Timothy Hennessy's house. *Confection maison : tableaux et étoffes faits main dans la demeure de Timothy Hennessy.* Handgefertigt: Selbst gemalte Bilder und Stoffe im Haus von Timothy Hennessy.

102/103 A gem: a Syrian mirror with mother-of-pearl on one of the Dodecanese islands. *Bijou : un miroir syrien nacré, sur une île du Dodécanèse.* Schmuckstück: Ein syrischer Spiegel mit Perlmutt auf einer Insel der Dodekanes.

104/105 Greek homeliness and French finesse: a living-room on Patmos. *Intimité grecque et finesse française : un salon à Patmos.* Griechische Gemütlichkeit und französische Finesse: Ein Salon auf Patmos.

106/107 Source of heat: a white faience oven in a private house on Patmos. *Source de chaleur : un four blanc en faïence dans une maison privée de Patmos.* Wärmequelle: Ein weißer Fayence-Ofen in einem Privathaus auf Patmos.

108/109 Meeting point: dining-room in a 17th century house. *Point de rencontre : salle à manger dans une maison du XVIIᵉ siècle.* Treffpunkt: Esszimmer in einem Haus aus dem 17. Jahrhundert.

110/111 Simple atmosphere: naive art and furniture made of untreated wood. *Atmosphère simple : art naïf et mobilier en bois non traité.* Schlichte Atmosphäre: Naive Kunst und Möbel aus unbehandeltem Holz.

112/113 Cotton canopy: a small bedroom with four-poster and chandelier. *Dais en coton : une petite chambre avec lit à baldaquin et lustre.* Baldachin aus Baumwolle: Ein kleiner Schlafraum mit Himmelbett und Kronleuchter.

114/115 Focal point: a bed in front of unplastered walls. *Au centre : lit devant des murs rustiques nus.* Im Mittelpunkt: Ein Bett vor unverputzt-ländlichen Mauern.

"…On the bottom of the box is a painting: a small coloured miniature of a girl from the last century. There's something magical in her expression, curls frame her pale noble face, her dress leaves her shoulders bare…"

Odysseas Elytis, in *ANOIXTA XAPTIA*

«…Sur le fond de la boîte se trouve une image : une petite miniature en couleur d'une fillette du siècle passé. Son expression a quelque chose de magique, des boucles encadrent un visage noble et pâle, sa robe dégagé ses épaules…»

Odysseas Elytis, dans *ANOIXTA XAPTIA*

»…Auf dem Boden der Dose ist ein Bild: eine kleine Farbminiatur eines Mädchens aus dem vergangenen Jahrhundert. Etwas Magisches geht von ihrem Ausdruck aus, Haarlocken umrahmen ein blasses edles Gesicht, das Kleid gibt die Schultern frei…«

Odysseas Elytis, in *Die Träume*

DETAILS

Details Details

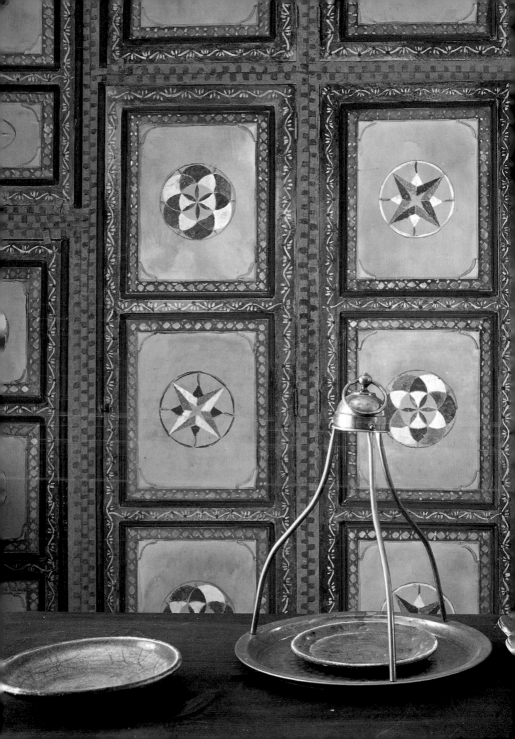

122 Out of water: a wrought-iron fish on Patmos. *Au sec : poisson en fer forgé sur Patmos.* Auf dem Trockenen: Ein schmiedeeiserner Fisch auf Patmos.

124 Knock, knock: a typically Greek blue door. *Bruits heurtés : une porte de maison en bleu typique de la Grèce.* Klopfgeräusche: Haustür in typisch griechischem Blau.

125 A guard: a knocker based on an ancient model. *Poste de garde : heurtoir d'après modèle antique.* Wachposten: Ein Türklopfer nach antikem Vorbild.

126 Glowing: the radiant, white-washed church on Seriphos. *Force lumineuse : église badigeonnée d'un blanc éclatant, à Seriphos.* Leuchtkraft: Die strahlend weiß getünchte Kirche von Seriphos.

128 Blue frame: on the "plateia" on Seriphos. *Cadre bleu : sur la « plateia » de Seriphos.* Blauer Rahmen: Auf der »plateia« von Seriphos.

129 Wall decorations: photographs and pictures in the tavern on Seriphos. *Décoration murale colorée : photos et tableaux dans la taverne de Seriphos.* Bunter Wandschmuck: Fotos und Bilder in der Taverne von Seriphos.

130 Room with a view: of Hydra; seen from the villa "Kourmada". *Chambre avec vue sur l'extérieur, à Hydra ; depuis la villa « Kourmada ».* Zimmer mit Ausblick: Blick über Hydra; von der Villa »Kourmada« aus gesehen.

132 A glass cross: in Vassily Tseghis' house on Seriphos. *Croix en verre : dans la maison de Vassily Tseghis à Seriphos.* Ein Kreuz aus Glas: Im Haus von Vassily Tseghis auf Seriphos.

133 A wooden cross: in Panos Alexopoulos' house on Seriphos. *Croix en bois : chez Panos Alexopoulos à Seriphos.* Ein Kreuz aus Holz: Bei Panos Alexopoulos auf Seriphos.

134 Soft back-rests: cushions in Panos Alexopoulos' living-room. *Coussins pour le dos : dans le salon de Panos Alexopoulos.* Kissen im Rücken: Im Wohnzimmer von Panos Alexopoulos.

136 Dove of peace: on a porcelain tureen in Vassily Tseghis' house. *Colombe de la paix : sur une terrine en porcelaine chez Vassily Tseghis.* Friedenstaube: Auf einer Porzellanterrine bei Vassily Tseghis.

137 Collectibles: vessels of all kinds in Vassily Tseghis' house. *Passion de collectionneur : récipients de toutes sortes dans la maison de Vassily Tseghis.* Sammelleidenschaft: Gefäße aller Art im Haus von Vassily Tseghis.

138 The roar of the sea: a shell in Panos Alexopoulos' house on Seriphos. *Ça gronde la mer : coquillage chez Panos Alexopoulos à Seriphos.* Das Meer rauschen hören: Eine Muschel bei Panos Alexopoulos auf Seriphos.

140 Chill out: comfortable sofas in pastel shades; at Vassily Tseghis' house. *Chill out: sofas confortables et tons pastels chez Vassily Tseghis.* Chill out: Gemütliche Sofas in Pastelltönen; bei Vassily Tseghis.

141 Portrait of a man: an engraving in Vassily Tseghis' house. *Image d'un homme: une gravure dans la maison de Vassily Tseghis.* Ein Bild von einem Mann: Eine Gravur im Haus von Vassily Tseghis.

142 Natural art: tulips in the former governor's palace. *Naturellement artificiel: tulipes dans l'ancien palais du gouverneur.* Natürlich künstlich: Tulpen im ehemaligen Palast des Statthalters.

144 With patina: a floor vase in the ancient style at Nikos Kostopoulos' house. *Patiné: un vase de style antique chez Nikos Kostopoulos.* Mit Patina: Eine Bodenvase im antiken Stil bei Nikos Kostopoulos.

145 Sea treasures: starfish and shells on a door in Nikos Kostopoulos' house. *Trésors de la mer: étoile de mer et coquillage sur une porte chez Nikos Kostopoulos.* Schätze des Meeres: Seestern und Muschel an einer Tür bei Nikos Kostopoulos.

146 Enthroned: a Victorian chair in Panos Alexopoulos' home on Seriphos. *Tel un trône: fauteuil victorien chez Panos Alexopoulos à Seriphos.* Wie ein Thron: Ein viktorianischer Sessel bei Panos Alexopoulos auf Seriphos.

148 Mirrored: still-life with stones. *Réflexion: nature morte avec pierres.* Gespiegelt: Stillleben mit Steinen.

149 At anchor: a small model of a ship decorating the wall. *A jeté l'ancre: petite maquette de bateau en décoration murale.* Vor Anker gegangen: Ein kleines Schiffsmodel als Wandschmuck.

151 Under the chandelier: a marvellous four-poster bed. *Sous le lustre: superbe lit à baldaquin.* Unterm Kronleuchter: Prachtvolles Himmelbett.

152 Well-observed: souvenirs at Nikos Kostopoulos' home. *Bien observé: Souvenirs dans la maison de Nikos Kostopoulos.* Gut beobachtet: Souvenirs im Haus von Nikos Kostopoulos.

153 Gathered: flotsam and jetsam as objects d'art. *Ramassé: morceaux d'épaves devenus objets design.* Aufgelesen: Strandgut als Designobjekte.

155 Refuge: a cosy bedroom. *Refuge: une chambre à coucher confortable.* Refugium: Ein gemütliches Schlafzimmer.

156 An oriental touch: a vase in Vassily Tseghis' weekend house. *Connotations orientales: vase dans la maison de campagne de Vassily Tseghis.* Orientalischer Anklang: Vase im Wochenendhaus von Vassily Tseghis.

157 Relaxing: on Miriam Frank's couch on Seriphos. *Détente: sur le canapé de Miriam Frank à Seriphos.* Entspannend: Auf der Couch von Miriam Frank auf Seriphos.

159 Two icons: Mary and Jesus above a sofa in Timothy Hennessy's house. *Deux icônes: Marie et Jésus au-dessus d'un sofa chez Timothy Hennessy à Hydra.* Zwei Ikonen: Maria und Jesus über einem Sofa bei Timothy Hennessy.

160 On the move: a rocking-chair at the home of Miriam Frank on Seriphos. *En mouvement: chaise à bascule chez Miriam Frank à Seriphos.* In Bewegung: Ein Schaukelstuhl bei Miriam Frank auf Seriphos.

161 Memories: sepia photographs in the for mer farmhouse "Langada" on Patmos. *Souvenirs sépia: photos dans l'ancienne maison paysanne «Langada» à Patmos.* Erinnerungen in Sepia: Fotos im ehemaligen Bauernhaus »Langada« auf Patmos.

162 Slim line: a vase in "Kourmada" on Hydra. *Silhouette élancée: un vase dans la maison «Kourmada» sur Hydra.* Schlanke Silhouette: Eine Vase im Haus »Kourmada« auf Hydra.

164 Winged sphinx: part of a gate on Hydra. *Ailé: le sphinx, détail d'une grille de porte à Hydra.* Beflügelt: Die Sphinx als Detail eines Torgitters auf Hydra.

165 In a cage: wall decoration in Panos Alexopoulos' house on Seriphos. *En cage: décoration murale chez Panos Alexopoulos à Seriphos.* Im Käfig: Wanddekoration bei Panos Alexopoulos auf Seriphos.

166 Round the corner: at Miriam Frank's house on Seriphos. *Pensé en coin: dans la maison de Miriam Frank à Seriphos.* Um die Ecke gedacht: Im Haus von Miriam Frank auf Seriphos.

168 Layered: shapely shells, fresh from the beech. *En couches: coquillages aux belles formes, venant de la plage.* Schichtarbeit: Formschöne Muscheln; direkt vom Strand.

169 Terracotta work: a relief in Vassily Tseghis' weekend house on Hydra. *En terracotta: un relief dans la maison de campagne de Vassily Tseghis à Hydra.* Aus Terrakotta: Ein Relief im Wochenendhaus von Vassily Tseghis auf Hydra.

170 A niche: the inner courtyard of a house on one of the Dodecanese islands. *Niche: dans la cour intérieure d'une maison sur une île du Dodécanèse.* Nischenplatz: Im Innenhof eines Hauses auf einer Insel der Dodekanes.

172 Simply beautiful: Marilena Liakopoulos' bathroom on Patmos. *Simple et beau: dans la salle de bain de Marilena Liakopoulos à Patmos.* Schön schlicht: Im Badezimmer von Marilena Liakopoulos auf Patmos.

173 Embroidered: the inhabitants of the sea. *Broderie: les habitants de la mer.* Auf Stoff gestickt: Die Bewohner des Meeres.

174 Art in the kitchen: colourful accents at the home on Hydra. *De l'art dans la cuisine: accents de couleur dans la maison à Hydra.* Kunst in der Küche: Bunte Akzente im Haus auf Hydra.

176 Rosy times ahead: blossoms on the window sill. *Le temps des roses: fleurs parfumées sur rebord de fenêtre.* Rosige Zeiten: Duftende Blüten auf dem Fenstersims.

177 Green oasis: a hidden veranda on Patmos. *Un coin de verdure: véranda cachée à Patmos.* Im grünen Bereich: Eine versteckte Veranda auf Patmos.

178 Patterned: blue-and-white guestroom in a house on Patmos. *Mélange de motifs: chambre d'amis en blanc et bleu dans une maison de Patmos.* Mustermix: Weiß-blaues Gästezimmer in einem Haus auf Patmos.

180 Natural art: corals and shells against a blue wall. *Œuvres d'art de la nature: coraux et coquillages devant un mur bleu.* Kunstwerke aus der Natur: Korallen und Muscheln vor einer blauen Wand.

181 A perfect curve: a shell. *Dynamique parfaite: un coquillage.* Perfekter Schwung: Eine Muschel.

182 Neatly in a row: the interior of "Zorba's Tavern" on Seriphos. *Bien alignée: la vaisselle de la « Taverne de Zorba » à Seriphos.* In Reih und Glied: Die Ausstattung von »Zobra's Taverna« auf Seriphos.

184 Radiantly beautiful: bathroom in a house on one of the Dodecanese islands. *Rayonnante de beauté: fragment de salle de bain sur une île du Dodécanèse.* Strahlend schön: Im Badezimmer eines Hauses auf einer Insel des Dodekanes.

185 Radiant: the enamel painted door of Dina Nikolaou's house on Hydra. *Brillante: la porte émaillée de la maison de Dina Nikolaou à Hydra.* Glänzend: Die mit Emailfarbe gestrichene Haustür von Dina Nikolaou auf Hydra.

187 Bright motifs: on the kitchen cupboards. *Motifs multicolores: ornant les placards de cuisine.* Bunte Motive: Auf den Küchenschränken.

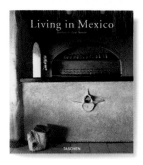 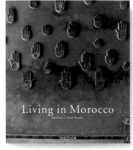 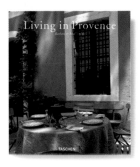

Living in Mexico
Ed. Angelika Taschen / Barbara &
René Stoeltie / Hardcover, 200 pp. /
€ 19.99 / $ 24.99 / £ 14.99 /
¥ 3.900

Living in Morocco
Ed. Angelika Taschen / Barbara &
René Stoeltie / Hardcover, 280 pp. /
€ 19.99 / $ 24.99 / £ 14.99 /
¥ 3.900

Living in Provence
Ed. Angelika Taschen / Barbara &
René Stoeltie / Hardcover, 200 pp. /
€ 19.99 / $ 24.99 / £ 14.99 /
¥ 3.900

"This book is absolutely yummy at a ridiculously cheap price. As much about architecture and design as travel – I defy you to say no." —*The Bookseller*, London on *Living in Provence*

"Buy them all and add some pleasure to your life."

African Style
Ed. Angelika Taschen

Alchemy & Mysticism
Alexander Roob

All-American Ads 40ˢ
Ed. Jim Heimann

All-American Ads 50ˢ
Ed. Jim Heimann

All-American Ads 60ˢ
Ed. Jim Heimann

Angels
Gilles Néret

Architecture Now!
Ed. Philip Jodidio

Art Now
Eds. Burkhard Riemschneider,
Uta Grosenick

Atget's Paris
Ed. Hans Christian Adam

Berlin Style
Ed. Angelika Taschen

Chairs
Charlotte & Peter Fiell

Christmas
Steven Heller

Design of the 20ᵗʰ Century
Charlotte & Peter Fiell

Design for the 21ˢᵗ Century
Charlotte & Peter Fiell

Devils
Gilles Néret

Digital Beauties
Ed. Julius Wiedemann

Robert Doisneau
Ed. Jean-Claude Gautrand

East German Design
Ralf Ulrich / Photos: Ernst
Hedler

Egypt Style
Ed. Angelika Taschen

M.C. Escher

Fashion
Ed. The Kyoto Costume
Institute

HR Giger
HR Giger

Grand Tour
Harry Seidler,
Ed. Peter Gössel

Graphic Design
Ed. Charlotte & Peter Fiell

Greece Style
Ed. Angelika Taschen

Halloween Graphics
Steven Heller

Havana Style
Ed. Angelika Taschen

Homo Art
Gilles Néret

Hot Rods
Ed. Coco Shinomiya

Hula
Ed. Jim Heimann

Indian Style
Ed. Angelika Taschen

India Bazaar
Samantha Harrison,
Bari Kumar

Industrial Design
Charlotte & Peter Fiell

Japanese Beauties
Ed. Alex Gross

Krazy Kids' Food
Eds. Steve Roden,
Dan Goodsell

Las Vegas
Ed. Jim Heimann

London Style
Ed. Angelika Taschen

Mexicana
Ed. Jim Heimann

Mexico Style
Ed. Angelika Taschen

Morocco Style
Ed. Angelika Taschen

**Extra/Ordinary Objects,
Vol. I**
Ed. Colors Magazine

**Extra/Ordinary Objects,
Vol. II**
Ed. Colors Magazine

Paris Style
Ed. Angelika Taschen

Penguin
Frans Lanting

20ᵗʰ Century Photography
Museum Ludwig Cologne

Pin-Ups
Ed. Burkhard Riemschneider

Photo Icons I
Hans-Michael Koetzle

Photo Icons II
Hans-Michael Koetzle

Pierre et Gilles
Eric Troncy

Provence Style
Ed. Angelika Taschen

Pussycats
Gilles Néret

Safari Style
Ed. Angelika Taschen

Seaside Style
Ed. Angelika Taschen

Albertus Seba. Butterflies
Irmgard Müsch

**Albertus Seba. Shells &
Corals**
Irmgard Müsch

South African Style
Ed. Angelika Taschen

Starck
Ed Mae Cooper, Pierre Doze,
Elisabeth Laville

Surfing
Ed. Jim Heimann

Sweden Style
Ed. Angelika Taschen

Sydney Style
Ed. Angelika Taschen

Tattoos
Ed. Henk Schiffmacher

Tiffany
Jacob Baal-Teshuva

Tiki Style
Sven Kirsten

Tuscany Style
Ed. Angelika Taschen

Web Design: Best Studios
Ed. Julius Wiedemann

Women Artists
in the 20ᵗʰ and 21ˢᵗ Century
Ed. Uta Grosenick

ICONS